The GOD DOG CONNECTION

*Things I've Learned about God and Faith
from the Dogs and Cats in My Life.*

MARTI HEALY

Library of Congress Catalog Number 2003107625
ISBN 0-9704410-2-9
Printed in U.S.A.

Published through Sweet Pea Press
10 1/2 North Main Street
Zionsville, Indiana 46077
800-755-3706

Book and jacket design by Lori Fox.

Photos on pages 21, 23, 27, 29, 43 and 47 courtesy of Sherry Long.
Photo on page 55 courtesy of Margie Janes.

Dedicated to God and Pookey.

CONTENTS

Things I've Learned about God and Faith from the Dogs and Cats in My Life.

•⟶•

DEAR READER...

•:•——•:•

Thank you for your interest in this book. Let me explain how I came to write it. I love God and I love animals. But only recently did it occur to me that there was a real connection between these two passions.

During a Bible study class I was taking through my church, I stumbled onto this revelation when I was trying to better understand some of the concepts we were learning. I believe that we learn best when we take new information and put it into terms of a subject we already know. Since I know animals, I tried this process, and I was amazed at the many GOD-DOG connections I discovered.

Perhaps this is one of the most wonderful and powerful things about the animals that God has filled our world with: in addition to being great friends, they are earthly, tangible connections to Him.

So, at the encouragement of a (human) friend, I've put some of my observations together into this book to share with you. But please know that these are simply my own personal observations, opinions and ideas. I am not an animal expert or a theologian. These are just my personal views and interpretations.

Most of the "connections" I've included in this book are very simple and straight-forward. And, most of the stories I relate are equally simple and gentle. I think for those who are at the beginning of their walk in faith, they may provide some key lessons or insights. For those who are more mature in spiritual development, perhaps they'll offer a starting point for more in-depth exploration, or maybe they'll simplify a concept down to its most basic component. And for those who simply love animals, I hope these essays provide at least some enjoyment – or bring an added depth of understanding and a new twist of appreciation to animal behavior.

Of course, the most obvious GOD-DOG connection of all is that of "unconditional love." Both God and our dogs (and cats) love us without reservation, without condition, and far beyond what we believe is possible or what we think we probably deserve. And in this book, I've also tried to include some perhaps less expected and more thought-provoking observations as well.

I truly hope you enjoy this collection of GOD-DOG connection essays, and that they may give you a reason to contemplate God's plan for us in a new light. And the next time you see a dog, cat or other critter, maybe you'll stop and say "thanks" – if for nothing more, at least for the opportunity they offer us to love and be loved unconditionally right here on earth.

Most sincerely,

Marti Healy

Marti Healy

Author with Taffy, circa 1950.

- Pookey -

HELLO.

•:——•:•

I was sitting on the ground, weeding a flowerbed. I just happened to look up, and here came the most adorable little black and white mixed-breed dog, trotting right up my walkway toward me. She trotted right into my heart. Her name was Pookey.

From the day we met, Pookey and I were devoted to each other. There was no question about her moving in with me – it was simply meant to be. We were made for each other, and understood each other instinctively right from the start. And, for the rest of her life, we were each other's very best friend.

About seven years later, we were in the midst of one of the coldest, snowiest winters on record. My neighbor called because she'd found a cat, half-frozen from the brutal weather, desperately scrounging breadcrumbs she'd put out for the birds. Pookey and I went to see her, and immediately brought her home to live with us. Her name was Katie.

For the first few weeks, Katie talked almost constantly. She seemed achingly in need of communicating with me – to tell me all about herself and her struggles.

I've never known a more grateful animal, either. It took awhile for Katie and me to really bond. But since we have, she's become one of the most loving, sensitive cats I've ever known. And, intriguingly, her desperate "talking" has ceased completely. Now, she speaks very little. She just senses that I understand her.

Almost three years after Katie came to me, I found a small, black and white female cat waiting at my back gate when I came home from work. She politely asked for dinner, was fed, and then took me to meet her baby boy who was living under the tool shed next door. His name was Sparkey.

As soon as this mother cat knew I would watch out for and feed her son, she left. Sparkey stayed. But his fears and shyness kept him from trusting me enough to come live in the house with us for almost a year. Slowly, step-by-step, he learned about love and safety, trust and comfort, happiness and respect. Although he's still shy around strangers, now Sparkey is a very cuddly, silly, lovable sweetheart. He's one of the most responsive and affectionate cats I've ever known.

Each of these animals came into my life and my heart in a vastly different way. Yet none was or is less precious to me than another.

I believe we each come to God in different ways, as well. Some of us come to Him as children, some of us as adults. Sometimes we experience an immediate devotion; other times it takes awhile to build the bond. Some of us are brought to Him by others; some find our own way. Some come through joy; some out of desperation. And, when we arrive in His presence, I believe we each build our own unique relationship with God.

But the most important point is that no matter how we get there, no matter what kind of relationship we share with Him – we're all equally precious to God. We're all wanted. He makes a safe and loving home for each of us.

DON'T LEAVE HOME WITHOUT ME.

When I first took a dog named Pookey in to live with me full-time, she wanted to be with me *all* of the time. Of course, this was not possible and, when I had to be absent from her, she did not react well. In fact, she took to chewing things – books and shoes, mostly. A similar thing happened with Edith Ann, a cat we once had at the office where I worked. She was fine during the day when we were all there. But at night, left alone, Edith Ann would go nuts – getting into everything from food in the kitchen to trash cans to digging in plants (spewing dirt all over the floors). I know many people with pets have experienced similar situations.

According to experts, it's called "separation anxiety," and it's the animal's way of reacting to the extreme stress they're experiencing because of being separated from us. We, after all, are the center of their universe. We represent love, food, safety, companionship – all the good things in life. Without us near them, they don't know if they will ever see us again. Can you imagine how that must feel? The terrible loneliness, the debilitating fear. It's no wonder our suffering pets "run amok."

I think we humans experience a similar "separation anxiety" when we are out of God's presence. We're filled with loneliness and an undefined fear. We frantically try to compensate for our sense of emptiness by doing all sorts of destructive activity. We don't know what to do; and nothing alleviates the discomfort until we're back in harmony with our master.

The key difference is that, while *we* are the ones who typically have to leave and cause the anxiety for our pets, God never leaves *us* alone. *We* are the ones who choose to leave God's presence. We cause our own pain. We "run amok" on our own. Thankfully, God's always waiting – with an open door and open arms – for our return. And then, we can relax: We're home, together again.

MIND ME AND PLAY NICE WITH EACH OTHER.

I always seem to have an assortment of different animals living with me at any one time. For the most part, I only require two things of them: they must learn to mind me, and they must get along with each other. If they can do that, they get a pretty good deal – a safe, warm, dry house; they're allowed on all the furniture and can sleep on my bed with me; they get fed regularly, with extra treats, too; they have a large, fenced-in back yard to explore; they have toys of every description; and they get frequent walks or car rides, plus special games and trips. They also receive regular health care and *LOTS* of love and petting, back scratches and tummy rubs. Life at my house is, indeed, a pretty good deal.

Over the years, I've had stray dogs come stay with me for awhile, but if they couldn't keep from chasing the cats, I had to find other homes for them. I've also known a few animals that just wouldn't listen to me or mind what I said; they, too, had to go elsewhere. What a shame! Look at all they missed out on – just for not being able to comply with two basic requirements: to mind me and get along with each other.

Most Christians are taught that all God ever asks of us are two basic things: mind Him, and get along with each other. He asks only that we love and obey Him above all others – with all our hearts and minds – and He asks that we love each other as we love ourselves and treat each other as we would want to be treated. If we can do these two things for Him, look at all the good stuff we get in return. How sad that we just can't seem to get it right most of the time.

FOLLOW ME TO SAFETY.

I used to pet sit for a dog named "Trouble." (That's right, the name gives you an indication.) He was a delightful mixed breed, about the size of a standard wire-haired terrier. Trouble had a wonderful light-hearted personality – which was good, because he got through life solely on his charm. He was a dog of very little intelligence. In fact, it amazed me that he was even housebroken. You could look deeply into his big brown eyes and there would be nothing going on in there. Trouble epitomized the saying: "The lights are on, but nobody's home." And Trouble's "lights" used a very dim bulb.

One day, Trouble got out of my fenced-in back yard and immediately ran toward a fairly busy road. Of course, calling him to me did no good because he understood no human words or commands, and everything in life to Trouble was just a big game. This game was called "chase me"! He gleefully allowed me to get within a few feet of him, and then he would jump and leap and run just out of reach. It wasn't long before Trouble had crossed the road and was in danger of either running back into the street again, or taking off across an open field where I would have no chance of catching him.

Throughout this "game of chase," my own dog Pookey (who was, of course, the *smartest* dog in the world) seemed to be assessing the situation, and then she went into action. She and Trouble were great friends, and she knew exactly how to communicate with him. She was also part Border Collie and had inherent herding instincts. Within a few minutes, Pookey had gotten Trouble's attention, and had him quietly following her every move. Obeying my commands, she then led Trouble safely back across the road and into the fenced-in yard.

Doesn't this story sound exactly like what Jesus did for us? Unable to understand God because His instruction far surpassed our simple comprehension, Jesus came to our rescue. In human form, Jesus was "one of us." He spoke our language in terms we could understand. He became our best friend. By trusting and following Him, He continues to lead us to safety.

WHOSE POO?

In the 12 years that my life was filled with the joy of living with my dog Pookey, she occasionally had "accidents" on the rug. Usually, it was when I was late getting home or, as she got older, due to her health. Therefore, I couldn't be angry with her – and I never punished her for it. I just got washable rugs.

But Pookey's sense of right-and-wrong was strong. And she was, I'm sure, embarrassed by these occasional mishaps. So her solution was to retrieve some "poo" from the cats' litter box and place it carefully right next to her own indiscretion. Apparently, I was supposed to think that "the cat did it" – or, at least, that it was a group effort, not hers alone. Never mind the fact that there was litter stuck all over the cat stuff – or that the cats had never had a (real) rug incident. To Pookey's mind, she had solved the problem. She did not have to take sole responsibility for her actions.

I'm afraid that, too often, we try to "fool" God about our own mistakes – we refuse to take full responsibility for our wrongdoings. How silly we are that we think we're putting one over on Him. We go to great lengths to blame others – to drag in their actions in an effort to cover up our own messes. This is certainly a form of "bearing false witness," isn't it? And we're really only fooling ourselves.

I think we'd be much better off if we'd just own-up, take responsibility, and ask for forgiveness right away. After all, God knows the truth. God *always* knows the truth. And no amount of "poo" is going to change that.

I SEE YOU.

My dog Pookey used to love having visitors and houseguests – especially other dogs. She had her favorites, of course, and these were usually the ones who readily allowed her to be the alpha dog (the acknowledged leader).

Pookey had a full set of "house rules" that her guests had to follow, including when to eat, where to sleep and how to play. She always had to be the first through the door, the first to receive a treat, and the one to decide which toys they could play with. But the most important, non-negotiable, number-one rule that Pookey had was that no one ever sat or slept closer to me than she did. She was kindhearted and generous in all things, but this was a rule about which she felt very strongly – and there was no discussion.

One day when a frequent visitor was staying with us – a black cocker spaniel named Gretchen – I was watching television, while Pookey was in her preferred spot right next to my chair. I noticed Gretchen starting to approach me but suddenly veering away. Then she'd start to come over but turn back again. This action was repeated several times and I couldn't figure out what was going on. All the while, Pookey was lying quietly at my side.

A few minutes later, Gretchen came toward me
again and I peeked over the side of the chair at Pookey.
I discovered that Pookey was closely watching Gretchen and, as Gretchen came
near, without moving or making a sound, Pookey would bare her teeth and make
a "snarly face" at Gretchen. As Gretchen would veer away, Pookey would let her
face go back to normal. The warning snarly face was repeated over and over,
whenever Gretchen entered the forbidden zone.

I'll never forget the total embarrassment that engulfed Pookey when she saw me
looking at her over the arm of the chair. She knew she was caught doing something
she wasn't supposed to do. She was absolutely humiliated to realize that I could
see what she was doing all along.

How many times do we think God can't see us when we "make snarly faces" at
each other? Nothing overt, no real confrontations – but threatening and impolite
just the same. We know we're not supposed to do it. Isn't it time we realized that
God can see us? No matter how clever we think we're being, God is watching us
all the time. Hopefully, we're at least properly embarrassed.

THE SOUND OF MY VOICE.

I don't know about other animal lovers, but I talk to my dogs and cats all the time. Actually, I talk to all animals with whom I come into contact. But I hold full discussions with the cats and dogs who share my home. It often surprises me when people say they might talk to their dogs but not their cats. I've found that cats are every bit as receptive to good conversation.

Regardless of species, we greet each other hello and goodbye at the door; we wake up with a good morning greeting and say goodnight, sleep tight, at bedtime. And throughout the day and evening, I tell them all about my day, my thoughts, my feelings – and I ask about theirs. I tell them how much I love them. I compliment them on their achievements (as they do me on mine). Sometimes we tell jokes. Sometimes we sing and dance. And sometimes we cry together. Sometimes they have something to say in return, but mostly they like to listen. They are *excellent* listeners.

Most animal experts tell us that talking to pets is a good idea. They say that even if the animal can't understand your words (which I believe is rather naive), they simply like to hear the sound of your voice. In fact, this verbal communication is critical to forming strong bonds between all types of pets and their humans.

I think this is very much the same with prayer. After all, what is prayer except conversations with God? Shouldn't we begin and end each day with words to Him? Shouldn't we tell God about all our actions, thoughts and feelings of the day? Shouldn't we declare our love and praise Him? Shouldn't we laugh, sing, dance and cry together?

Sometimes God answers us right while we're speaking to Him; and sometimes not. But mostly I think He likes to just listen (another outstanding listener). So whether or not I get a response, I keep right on talking. Because, like my animals, I believe God just likes to hear the sound of my voice.

- Katie -

24

CUSTOMIZED LOVING.

•⋅——⋅•

One thing I've discovered over years of animal friendships is that, while each one needs constant love, they all seem to respond best if it's demonstrated on their own terms.

As examples of this observation, my dog Pookey was loyal to a fault, with unquestioning love for me. But she was not a cuddler. She preferred just being with me and hearing me talk to her. My cat Katie wants to sit on my lap or next to me constantly, but hates being held or lifted. And she can't tolerate being touched on her back. Sparkey, my other cat, wants to be held, cuddled, rocked, and cooed over like a baby – but only once or twice a day, and then only until he says he's had enough, thank you very much. Pepper, a dog I've known since he was a puppy, still likes to fall asleep in my arms, but otherwise doesn't like to be held or cuddled. I also once knew a cat that was so shy and uncertain that she only let you pet her with your bare feet. (Don't ask me how we knew this.)

But the point is that, for the most rewarding relationships, we need to show our love for animals in the way that makes them feel how much they're loved yet respected for their individual needs and comfort levels.

I believe God does this very same thing. I believe He loves each of us in the way we need it most.

In fact, this is my own interpretation of the Beatitudes in the Bible (i.e., *"Blessed are the meek, for they shall inherit the earth,"* etc.). A minister friend of mine once said that the original meaning of the term "blessed" is not the way we interpret it today; it doesn't mean "lucky." Rather, it means "praised" and I think we could add "respected." I used to think of the Beatitudes as sort of instructions for how to live, and the rewards we'd receive if we lived those ways (e.g., if you're meek, you'll inherit the earth). But now, I believe they're actually promises to us that God will respect our individual differences, and love us according to our needs.

Just like I express my love to my cat Katie: *"I respect the fact that you don't want your back touched, so I'll show my love for you by scratching your head or ears."* So God might say to one of us humans: *"I respect the fact that it's hard for you to trust other people, so I'll show my love for you by putting plenty of children and animals in your life."* Or *"I respect the fact that you love me and like to teach others, so I'll show my love for you by calling you to the ministry."*

I believe that this is what Jesus was saying in the Bible: "Blessed are the meek"...
(*"If you're meek and shy by nature, I'll respect that fact"*) ... "for they shall inherit the
earth"...(*"and so I'll show my love for you by one day letting you have everything your
heart desires, and you won't need to do anything or even ask, it will just come to you like
an inheritance."*)

Think what this means: God loves each of us in our own special way; and He
shows it by *customizing* His love for us according to our personal needs. Wow.

WHY ME?

One of the worst days of the year at my house is when the cats and/or dogs have to go to the vet for their annual immunizations and checkups. I, of course, know that it must be done, that it's for their own good. They, on the other hand, just know that they're having a perfectly good day when they wind up in a smelly, scary place and get stuck in the neck (or other parts) with sharp instruments, and are generally poked and prodded and touched in places they would prefer to keep private.

I feel so terribly guilty about it because I know they can't possibly understand what's going on and why I do it to them. They trust me, and I do "bad" things to them for no good reason in their opinion.

I often wish I could just explain what it's all about, but how could I describe the concept of immunization to them? The whole idea would be far beyond their ability to comprehend it. So I just try to build their trust in me, and know that what I'm doing is in their best interest. I stay right with them and try to help them get through it as easily and quickly as possible.

This must be what it's like for God. We're taught that God's plan far surpasses our human understanding – probably on the same scale that immunization is to cats and dogs.

We often question why "bad" things happen for no apparent reason. I believe that God would like to be able to explain it to us, too – but knows how far beyond our comprehension it would be. So He just hopes we learn to trust Him, and then He stands by us and tries to make our challenges and pain as easy and quick as possible.

- Toby -

CHOOSING WHERE TO LIVE.
·:——:·

Toby was the first cat to live with me when I was an adult on my own. She was independent, vain, strong-willed, very smart, and wished she could have lived with someone far "cooler" than I was.

Whenever she was bored or mad at me for some reason (like when I wouldn't let her sit out on the open window ledge of my apartment, three stories up), she would stamp her little feet, get a running start, jump up and grab hold of the apartment door handle with her front paws. There she would hang, thinking the door would surely open soon, and she could run away and go live across the hall with our neighbor (a cat lover and Toby's personal pawn). Thankfully, Toby was a tiny thing, without the body weight to actually turn the doorknob. But she was five pounds of solid ego.

Toby's world consisted of two categories of events: 1) Things that affected Toby; and 2) Things that didn't matter. She was a bed hog and a chair monopolizer. She wanted to taste everything I fixed for myself to eat, and she liked to play in my bathwater. She turned my entire apartment (and later my house) into one giant cat toy. She danced in the fireplace (ashes and all) and climbed the window shutters like a ladder. She was a rowdy little punk, and I loved her dearly.

But as much as I adored and indulged her, she would have readily gone to live with just about anyone else. I protected her from harm, kept her warm and well fed. I gave her the best of medical care and bought her toys of every description. I never raised my hand against her. And yet, I believe she would have left me for a stranger without a backward glance.

Of course, she didn't know there are those in this world who are not always kind to cats (especially self-centered ones). And she had never experienced the harsh realities of living on the streets. But if she could have managed to somehow twist open that front doorknob, I think I would have been history.

Are we sometimes as inconstant and disloyal to God? Aren't we sometimes easily tempted to run off with just about anyone or any spiritual concept or dogma that comes our way? It seems that no matter how good God is to us, we sometimes let ourselves become distracted by worldly and unworthy "masters." Perhaps it's because we don't realize the potential dangers we face in leaving God's protective care. And look how unhappy we make ourselves and all the energy we expend by trying to "run away" instead of simply appreciating and enjoying all that God has given us.

Toby never really had a choice about where she would live. Her "free will" was restricted by lack of body weight and no opposable thumbs. Our choice, however, is totally up to us. We all must decide for ourselves. Hopefully, we'll choose wisely and rightly – to dwell in the presence of the Lord.

I'VE GOT YOUR BACKSIDE.

I haven't had a bed all to myself for most of my adult life: every dog and cat who has ever lived or stayed at my house is allowed to sleep on my bed with me. Sometimes it gets a little crowded, and often hairy, but I wouldn't have it any other way.

Each critter picks his or her preferred spot; but almost invariably, an animal will position itself in a back-to-back, head-to-tail arrangement. This is the way they sleep in the wild with each other – and for a very practical reason. This way, they can each be protected from an unseen attacker from behind. It also provides a great deal of warmth. To be honest, I feel quite privileged to be so trusted and accepted "into the pack."

Another thing I've noticed is how much more secure I feel when there are animals around me at night. Before I had my first live-in dog Pookey, I suffered from recurring frightful dreams. And, often, I would lie awake late into the night too frightened to sleep or get up and investigate some creepy, unidentified noise. But with Pookey – as with other companion animals – I found I could sleep soundly and securely all through the night. I now know if a strange sound is worth any concern, my friends with the super senses will let me know.

In fact, Pookey was so protective of me while I slept that whenever I visited my parents, she would not allow even my mother to wake me in the morning. Pookey would position herself as bodyguard between me and anyone who entered the room, so Mom was only allowed to get within a certain distance from the bed. Pookey truly loved my mother – but while I was asleep, Pookey's instinctive job was to protect and watch over me, no matter what.

Many of us as children were taught to pray to God at night to protect us as we slept. But how many of us still do? I think we'd all probably sleep much better if we'd just put all our scary thoughts and worries into God's hands as we crawl into bed – and just know that He'll watch over us and take care of all our fears. We need to have faith that God's "got our backside." Then, we can sleep tight,
all through the night.

JUST LET IT GO.

When I was in the first grade, everyone in my class hand made ashtrays as Christmas gifts for our dads (this was over 50 years ago). For our moms, we made sprinkling bottles for dampening clothes before ironing (yes, indeed, an era now long departed). We even spent additional days and weeks crafting our own wrapping paper. These prized works of art were eventually carried home and placed lovingly and oh-so-carefully under the tree just days before Christmas.

That evening, while the family was away, our dog Taffy sorted through the packages, selected only these two, and tore and chewed them to bits. In the half century that has passed since then, I have never been so indescribably angry with any other animal.

Until then, Taffy had been the love of my life, my loyal pal and playmate. But my best friend had betrayed me and broken my six-year-old heart, and I was quite sure I would never, *ever* forgive him. I refused to speak to him or even look at him for days. And this reaction – from *his* best friend – must have wrenched his little heart in two as well.

Finally, after my temper had cooled, I allowed myself to at least look at him and acknowledge his presence. He looked soulfully back at me – and suddenly, we were hugging and dancing around on the kitchen floor.

I will always remember the complete flood of warmth and love that filled me at that very moment. I can only think that it must have been "unconditional forgiveness."

I believe that this is the way we need to accept forgiveness from God – completely and wholly, without reservation. Too often, I think we hold on to and nurture the old hurt. But as long as the pain and guilt and anger are taking up space in our hearts, there's no room for the forgiveness to flood in and fill the space. We need to just let it go . . . accept the forgiveness . . . unconditionally.

KEEP RINGING THE BELL.

Toby, my first cat, was smart as a whip and often bored. She was also very independent, taking the concept of "free will" to the level of an art form. And, bless her heart, she was quite manipulative – and proud of it.

Taking all of these personality traits into consideration, she and I worked out a system whereby she could "request" special kitty treats by ringing a service bell that I had found at a flea market. It was one of those countertop bells, with the button on top that could be tapped to make the bell "ding." We kept it on the kitchen counter.

She loved it. In record time, she learned to use it and would call me to the kitchen whenever she wanted a treat. (The dog quickly learned to come too: I mean, as long as you're handing out treats . . .)

To Toby's credit, she didn't usually overuse the bell. But sometimes, in the middle of the night, I could hear a faint "ding-ding, ding-ding-ding" coming from the kitchen. To *my* credit, I did *not* get up out of bed to indulge her cravings. Sometimes, too, when I returned home after being gone all day, I would notice that the bell had been moved across the counter (a result of strongly repeated ringings).

Some might term these futile, unrewarded bell ringings as simply conditioning or habit. But to me, they represented something else: a genuine "act of faith."

How often do we perform some act or request something from God, anticipating a certain response? But if the expected response isn't forthcoming, does our faith become diminished? I believe we have to invest all our faith, hope, trust and anticipation, and just keep on ringing that bell. Maybe we won't get a response that particular time . . . but, then again, maybe we will.

A PAW FOR A PAW.

At the present time, there are two cats living with me: Katie, the eldest, a long-haired, female, calico "princess"; and Sparkey, her assistant. Sparkey is a short-haired, black-and-white male, five years younger than Katie, and not terribly bright.

From the day Sparkey moved into the house, Katie has bossed him around and pretty much taken advantage of him. Sometimes she thinks he's mildly amusing. And sometimes she condescends to lick his head and wash his face. And if there is any perceived danger around (a stray cat, an aggressive dog, a bug with an attitude), Katie will leap to defend Sparkey from the threat. But for the most part, she merely tolerates him as "that new boy."

Toward the beginning of their relationship, however, when Sparkey was generally ignored by Katie, an incident occurred when Katie was accidentally stepped on by a human visitor. She let out a loud "yowl" that startled everyone – including Sparkey, who came running to see what all the fuss was about. The offending visitor immediately bent down to apologize to Katie and to make sure no real harm had been done. Like the true lady she is, Katie accepted the apology with grace, rubbed up against the visitor's leg, then strolled over to where Sparkey was innocently watching, and beat the tar out of him. Poor Sparkey could only blink and flinch and stagger backward in disbelief.

Animal and human behavior experts alike call this "misplaced aggression." And I'm sure this is part of what God meant in the Bible where it talks about "an eye for an eye" and "a tooth for a tooth." Just because someone hurts us – by accident or not – that doesn't give us the right to take out our anger and hurt and frustration on someone else. How many times do we experience pain in one part of our lives only to inflict it onto others who have had no responsibility for that hurt? How often do we get our foot stepped on and then "beat up" someone unrelated to that injury? But bless Sparkey's little heart – like the lesson taught by Jesus, he simply turned the other cheek and walked away.

BE A TEACHER.

A sweet, young, boy cocker spaniel named "Hollywood" came to stay with us while his family took a trip. Pookey, my ultra-wise, mixed-breed, girl dog, who loved playing hostess, thought Hollywood was the most fun house guest we had ever entertained.

Hollywood was just a baby, really, only a few months old. So he knew basically nothing about being a Proper Dog. Pookey took this as her cue to teach him everything. In one long weekend, she housebroke him, taught him how to drink water out of a hose, how to build a fort out of the woodpile, how to chase butterflies and eat bugs, how to dig a hole and bury a bone. She also instructed him about coming when you're called, respecting cats and defending civilization as we know it against UPS trucks. When Hollywood's mom and dad came to pick him up, they were amazed at his new-found maturity.

If Pookey hadn't been Hollywood's teacher, would he have learned all these things? I honestly don't know. I do know that puppies and kittens are remarkable

mimics. Although much comes to them through instinct, they learn many of their life skills by imitating examples from one of their own kind.

I believe this is the way God wants us to "witness" or minister about our faith to others – especially to our own little ones. We need to assume the responsibility of teaching our children ourselves, and not simply leave it to someone else or some institution. I think we need to be living examples to them – give them positive, faith-based, moral, role models to imitate. Christianity...religion...faith...these are always just one generation away from being lost forever. Our next generation needs us – no less than Hollywood needed Pookey – for gaining life skills and spiritual lessons, for learning about God and love and being the very best human beings we can be. (Bug eating, of course, is optional.)

DID YOU CALL?

One of the most basic lessons we teach our companion animal friends is to come when they're called, and for many very good reasons: to keep them from getting lost or left behind; to keep them away from danger; to be fed; to rest; to receive a favorite treat; to do something we need them to do; or simply to get a hug and keep us company.

Pookey, my all-time favorite dog, was especially prompt to come when she was called – except at bedtime. Coming in from that last romp in the yard at night was very, very hard for her. And as good and well-behaved as she was in every other situation, when she ignored my calling for her at night, it would make me rather angry and disappointed in her.

I think it's that way with God, too. When He calls us to something, it's for many very good reasons: to keep us from getting lost or left behind; to keep us away from danger; to be replenished when our spirit is hungry; to rest and refresh our souls; to receive some unexpected joy or unanticipated reward; to do something for Him – to be of service or ministry; or simply to receive His love and dwell for awhile in His company.

And no matter how good or mindful we might be in other ways, if we don't come when we're called, I'll bet it makes God pretty mad and disappointed in us, too.

Listen carefully...come when we're called...I suspect it's that simple.

HAVE FUN.

—

A human friend of mine is one of the best teachers of dogs I've ever known. One resulting example of her talent is Jesse, a 100-pound golden lab. My friend took this bouncy, bundle of pure energy and silliness and, with love and patience alone, turned her into a focused, respectful companion who is welcome almost anywhere.

I truly believe what animal experts tell us about the effects of such instruction: Because Jesse knows what's expected of her, and the rules she is supposed to follow, she is happier and more fulfilled than if she had received no training at all.

What surprises me most about the process is how few basic commands there are. With just a handful of rules, Jesse learned all the necessary guidelines for acceptable behavior.

Another intriguing element to me is that one of the basic commands for Jesse is the phrase: "Free puppy!" This tells her she's free to be on her own – she can romp and roll and be silly at will. Yet, even in this "free puppy" state, Jesse doesn't break the other rules. Now, they're simply a part of her natural behavior.

With just a handful of basic rules, God has given *us* all the necessary guidelines for living a happier, more fulfilled life. He calls them the Ten Commandments. Only ten. That certainly leaves a great deal open for our own discretion, doesn't it? With only ten basic rules, the rest is up to us – left to our own free will.

Taking that thought even further, I have come to believe that "free will" itself should be considered the "eleventh commandment." (Not unlike "free puppy" is an actual command for Jesse.) Think about it. The phrase "free puppy" doesn't mean a thing to a dog who hasn't had any instruction. And to a person who has no familiarity with or doesn't follow the Ten Commandments, the concept of free will has little or no meaning. But for those of us who do respect and try to keep the Commandments – to those of us who make them a natural part of our behavior – "free will" could be God's actual commandment to us to truly enjoy our lives on this beautiful earth He has made for us. I believe He wants us to occasionally romp and roll and be silly at will. What fun!

- Pepper with his brothers and sisters -

THE "BINKY."

It was the hottest summer I could remember in years. Two stray dogs showed up at my office building – a boy and a girl. Of course, I had to bring them home with me – I couldn't leave them to suffer in the heat – lost, alone and unprotected. And (of course), the little girl dog was going to have puppies – soon. Two weeks later, she delivered seven sets of the sweetest, tiniest, toes, ears and tails you could imagine. It took six months, but eventually all nine (mom, dad and seven babies) were placed in loving, appropriate homes. I still exchange Christmas cards with many of the families.

The last little guy to find his permanent home was Pepper. Pepper was a dog's dog – a pup's pup. The world was his playground, and everything in it was a toy. With six littermates, he was the first to start a rough and tumble game in the morning and the last to give it up at night. In fact, it was his inherent rowdiness that took him out of the running of the initial adoption opportunities.

As his playmate options diminished over the weeks and months (one-by-one, they packed and moved to their new families' homes), Pepper soon turned his attention to the two house cats as potential "best friends."

Female cat Katie let him know that she was not available for the role. Sparkey, the easily intimidated male cat, didn't seem to have a say in the matter.

Pepper would seek Sparkey out at every opportunity, grasp him by the scuff of the neck, and drag him all around the house like his own personal "Binky." Sparkey, for his part, would fold up his legs and tail and assume a prenatal position while letting out pitiful little weak cries of *"help me, help me, puleeeeze..."*

Although I could see that Pepper was doing no physical harm to Sparkey, in response to Sparkey's obvious emotional distress, I would intervene and separate them. Upon being emancipated, Sparkey would take refuge in a dog-free zone of the house for awhile, and Pepper would have to settle for a non-living squeak-toy. This went on for weeks.

One day, however, when Pepper was lazily dozing in the sun, I caught Sparkey going up to him and flopping down in front of Pepper's muzzle. He was pushing the back of his neck right up into Pepper's face, and making squeaky sounds, actually inviting Pepper to grab hold and begin the "dragging my Binky" routine.

But, as soon as Pepper complied, it was *"help me, help me, puleeeeze"* all over again.

How often do we willingly put ourselves in harm's way, only to then desperately ask God to "save us" from the danger? Many of us repeatedly participate in a multitude of ill-advised, risky behaviors, and then panic and turn to God for rescuing when we get scared. How many times do we think God should fall for this? If we're going to act like "Binkies," we probably shouldn't be surprised when we get dragged across the floor. And, after deliberately choosing to take such risks, over and over again – without changing or repenting at all – I don't think we really have the right to keep asking God to *"help me, puleeeeze."* Do you? Well, God does. Surprisingly . . . fortunately . . . lovingly . . . God does.

- Sparkey -

WHERE ARE YOU?

I came home rather late after work one night. Katie, my faithful female cat companion came running to greet me at the door as usual. I typically had to call Sparkey to come – the shy, young male cat who had only recently moved into the house from a near-feral lifestyle outside.

I called – several times – with no response. After I searched the house and all his favorite hideaways, Sparkey was still nowhere to be found. Then, with a sinking feeling in my stomach, I saw the torn window screen. This open window was a favorite napping place for Sparkey; apparently, after months of leaning against it, his body weight had finally caused the screen to give-way. And, naturally, he decided to take the opportunity to go exploring. Thankfully, Katie hadn't followed.

I rushed outside and started calling and calling – but no Sparkey. It had taken me almost a full year to get Sparkey tamed enough to move into the house full-time. During that year, he had lived primarily in the crawlspace under my house, where it was at least warm and dry and I could feed and watch out for him. But when he finally moved into the house itself, I kept him in – where it was much safer, cleaner and more comfortable. He had seemed perfectly content. But now he was lost – out in the elements – alone and unprotected.

It was getting dark and I was running out of places to look – but I kept calling. I could see Katie watching me from inside the house. I knew she was waiting for her supper, but all I could think about was finding my poor, lost, little Sparkey. He was so shy – and must be so frightened by now. My throat felt tight and my stomach was knotted.

Just as I was beginning to feel the cold fear that he might be lost forever, I heard his cry – soft and faint, but unmistakably his. It was coming from the crawlspace underneath the house. Of course! The one outdoor place he remembered as being "safe."

Sure enough, in a corner against one wall, he was huddled and calling for me. When he saw me, he came running into my arms.

Safely back in the house, Katie and I both fawned over him, and we all shared a very happy dinnertime.

Total elapsed time: approximately 17 minutes.

I guess it doesn't matter to God, either, how long someone goes missing; if one is lost, it's simply a time of great anguish – whether that's minutes or years. And whether one "falls" out or chooses to run away doesn't seem to matter as well.

Like Sparkey, some of us who have become lost, simply can't find our own way back – even when we want to. Fortunately (also like Sparkey), all we have to do is call – and we will be found. God will come find us and He will lead us back home again in His arms.

Prodigal cat...prodigal son. Lost kitty...lost sheep...lost souls. Whoever is lost is the one who is actively sought and pursued. But back home where we belong, everyone shares in a very happy celebration.

GET OUT OF THE WAY, PLEASE.

Apparently, I can be a real creature of habit – highly predictable. At least this was the opinion held by Pookey, my faithful little dog.

For instance, every night when I arrived home from work, there would of course be the obligatory greetings at the door and scramble to the back yard for immediate relief. But then Pookey would race back into the house and upstairs into my bedroom. Here, she would wait by my closet for me to change clothes; then, she would run to the bathroom sink and wait while I washed my hands; and finally, she would leap back downstairs into the kitchen where she would sit beside her bowl and wait for dinner to be served. Like clockwork: hello . . . outside . . . bedroom . . . bathroom . . . kitchen . . . dinner. If I stopped to read the mail or the phone rang, it totally threw her off her game.

In fact, Pookey liked to "predict" my movements as much as possible – in or outside of the house. Rather disturbingly, she was frequently right. But, quite often, she was *not* able to correctly anticipate where I was going. On these occasions, she might wind up in the wrong room, or upstairs when I was down, or in the garage while I was in the garden. Sometimes, she even walked into furniture, fences or cats while she was watching me over her shoulder in an effort to stay ahead of me. Even these embarrassments didn't deter her from trying, though. All her life, Pookey's goal was to "anticipate" where I was going and what I wanted, rather than just waiting to follow me.

I think we're sometimes tempted to do the same thing with God. Sometimes we're so sure we know exactly what God has planned, that we run headlong in front of Him, without waiting for directions.

But trying to always "anticipate" God's desire can be rather risky. (And I'm guessing it makes God a little nervous, too.) This is how people trek off down the wrong path, or wind up way off in a field – while God's back in the garden. We also take the chance of running into something dangerous and hurting ourselves, or becoming separated from God altogether, or – worse yet – hurting others in the process.

Wouldn't it be smarter to just *follow* God? Perhaps we should stop trying to anticipate God, step out of the way, and just let Him take the lead.

TALKING THROUGH THE HEART.

The way my house is configured, I have one outside entrance door that is at a 90-degree angle to and about 15 feet away from another outside entrance door. In good weather, I typically keep both doors open, with the screen doors latched, so that all resident cats, dogs and I can remain inside while still enjoying the fresh air.

Recently, while two dogs were my temporary houseguests, my cat Katie discovered an interesting acoustical phenomenon involving these doors. When she made a particular "yowl" out through the east door, the sound traveled back in through the north door – sounding exactly as if there were a cat in the bushes just outside the north side of the house. It drove the dogs nuts.

The sound she made was one of "distress." Since I knew she was not actually in distress, I could only assume she somehow knew exactly what she was doing. And, intriguingly, she had determined that this sound evoked the most passion from the dogs. They became very agitated in their desire to find "the yowling cat in the bushes" (which the latched screen prevented them from doing). Katie seemed to take such delight in her version of a ventriloquism act that I didn't have the heart to enlighten her two fall-guys to the truth about the "bush cat."

Katie's "distress call" is just one of a variety of voices she and all cats and dogs use to communicate vocally. From the sound alone, I typically can tell when one of mine is hurt, happy, angry, trapped, being silly, afraid, hungry, wanting to play, wanting a hug, wanting just to talk, sad, cranky, tired, startled, or just plain bored. Without a spoken word, I know what they need or want, because I know *them*, because I love them so much. I listen to them with my heart.

Without a word, I think God knows our every need, too. Just by the sound of our voices, I believe He knows whether we need comfort or inspiration, a place to hide or a place to grow, whether we need help or want to say thanks. Even when we go to God not knowing what we need or want or what to say, not even knowing how to put our thoughts and feelings into words, I believe God knows – because He knows *us*, and because He loves us so much. I guess all we really need to do is just talk to God through our hearts.

PLEASE SHARE MY CHAIR.

In my living room there is a large, over-stuffed armchair. This is where I end most of my days, to read or watch television, surrounded by my furry companions. The back and arms of the chair are wide and well rounded – the perfect size and shape for cats (and some adventurous small dogs) to stretch out on and get a little up-close-and-personal attention.

The chair seat is also quite wide, and (particularly in cooler weather) my younger male cat Sparkey sometimes likes to settle down on the seat to one side of me for some even closer-up personal cuddling. When he does, Katie, the older female cat, perches herself on the chair arm, mildly staring down at Sparkey. One-by-one, she slowly stretches out her legs over the side, "accidentally" poking Sparkey in the back. Eventually, she leaps over to my lap (oops...did I kick you in the head, Sparkey?), and then flops down heavily across my legs. Her plentiful backside soon slips off the side of my lap and just happens to cover up Sparkey's entire head and neck. He can't see, hear or breathe. Mission accomplished.

Even when Sparkey doesn't just give up and move away, Katie believes herself to be "the winner" because she's managed to obtain the prime position – right next to me. And yet, throughout all the maneuvering and manipulation, there is still room to spare. There are *two* arms to that chair, a wide back, space on *either* side of my lap, as well as my lap itself. I have plenty of chair and attention to go around, but sharing is apparently never considered.

Does this sound familiar? Does it remind us of something or someone? Countries? Nations? Races? Governments? Religions? Beliefs? God has given us a very big chair. And He has enough love and attention for *everyone*. So this is what I suspect God is wondering: Why can't we share? Why can't we all just . . . share?

- Butch -

IS IT MINE?
·:———·:·

Butch is a big ol' dog. A real, old-fashioned, in-your-face, good ol' boy. He's part golden lab; all male; all dog. Butch doesn't just enter a room or yard, he bursts onto the scene. He has a tremendous amount of personality and a lot of heart, but very little class.

Butch lives in the house right behind mine. I think he's terrific. And, for all his indelicacy, the cats, quite surprisingly, like him too.

Our pal Butch comes over to visit us almost every day. I keep special rawhide chewbones, toys and biscuits handy for him. Regrettably, however, I usually can't allow Butch to stay very long on these visits because he has an unfortunate outlook on life. To Butch, everything is "mine."

In dog terms, the territorial claims process involves leaving as much of your scent as possible (urine works best) on everything – inside and out. Furniture, floors, doors, bushes, birdbaths, flowers, fenceposts, stairs, potted plants – even my shoes and the cats themselves have, at one time or another, been marked by Butch as "mine." And then, of course, each item and place must be re-marked at every opportunity. (The cats still like him, but they've learned to duck.)

A somewhat less startling but equally unfortunate way Butch has of protecting "his" property and making sure he retains all rights to it is to bury it. This way, he can keep it hidden until later when he might have a need for it. It's the fate of many of the chewbones. (So far, the cats have escaped this particular act of ownership.)

Poor Butch. If he would only just enjoy the beauty of the flowerbeds and plants . . . if he could simply take pleasure in the shade of the trees, the comfort of the house, and the friendship of the cats . . . if he would only realize there is plenty of yard and house for everyone to share . . . without having to "own" it all. But his desperate acts to claim everything as "mine" actually damage the very things he is trying to keep to himself. Eventually, it even results in his being cast out.

Remember Adam and Eve? As a child, I was taught in Sunday School that the infamous apple was a test of Adam and Eve's obedience to God. Might it also have been a lesson in good stewardship?

I believe the whole reason God gave us "dominion" over all the earth and animals and plants and other natural resources was not so we could claim them as "mine." I think He gave them to us so we could take care of them. We are, after all, the only presence on earth that has the *ability* to take care of everything else on earth. I wonder why we find it so hard to believe we have the *responsibility* to do so.

Since Adam and Eve, we've eaten an awful lot of apples. And we've dug plenty of holes. We've also spent a great deal of time and effort "marking" territory. The thing is, none of it is "ours." It's God's. Everything belongs to God. I think it's time we realized we've simply been given the privilege of taking care of it on His behalf.

LISTEN.

One morning, my best human friend stopped over just to say hello. We were standing in the kitchen talking, when Katie, my older female cat, came in to greet our visitor. Pleasantries were exchanged and my friend and I continued our conversation.

Sparkey, my younger male cat, then walked into the kitchen. My friend greeted him. No response. I said, "Look who's here, Sparkey." No response. My friend called to him and whistled. No response. Sparkey continued to walk slowly and aimlessly around the kitchen, tail at half-mast, shoulders and ears relaxed, a simple little tune running through his head...dum, diddle-dum, diddle-dee. Sparkey – whose vision, hearing and other senses are perfectly normal – was totally oblivious to anyone else's presence. He was in Sparkey's world. It's a place he goes to frequently.

Another of my animal friends had a similar habit. Pookey, my long-time dog companion, used to set time aside every evening at dusk. As long as weather permitted, she would sit quietly on the back porch steps and contemplate. As the fireflies and crickets came to life, she would listen to soft, faraway sounds – distant music, voices from the next block over, a faint barking from the farm down the road. She would savor the twilight smells – warm earth, fragrant blooms, tomato plants, cut grass. She would be still and silent and simply sit "in the moment."

I admire Pookey and Sparkey tremendously for their ability and determination to do this. They, like all animals I've noticed, deliberately and purposefully take the time to have these quiet moments of reflection on a regular basis.

Do you suppose they could be listening for the voice of God? Do we listen for God? Do we set time aside each day to sit quietly and listen for that "still, small voice" that is described in the Bible sometimes as a "whisper"? Or do we try to fill every minute of every day with conversations and work and entertainment – computers and cell phones and television and music and movies?

Since God doesn't typically use call waiting or e-mail, I think He's hoping we'll take a cue from our animal examples. Let me suggest that, for just a few minutes every day, we sit silently on the back porch steps at dusk, or walk softly into the kitchen, or turn off the phones, the T.V., the computer, and be hushed and just listen...listen for that "still, small voice" from God.

BE TRUE TO YOURSELF...BE TRUE TO GOD.

I always believed my sweet and loving little dog Pookey was part Border Collie. Pookey, on the other hand, always believed she was part cat. Perhaps this was because she was raised with a litter of cats, with no other dogs around. Of course, she thought she was inexplicably large for a cat. But she faithfully retained and practiced her cat ways all her life: she licked her paw and washed her face regularly; and she tried hard to "purr" while she was being petted. Regretfully, her "purring" almost always resulted in a sound that was a cross between a snort, a snarl and a sinus condition, so people unfamiliar with her self-image sometimes found it off-putting.

Currently, my lovable cat Sparkey has an equally unique image of himself. (We're not quite sure what it is.) In the mornings, as I'm brushing my hair and putting on my makeup, Sparkey climbs into my lap and then up onto the dressing table. Here, he positions himself between me and the mirror and begins pawing through the makeup box. Some days, he refuses to move and gets quite belligerent until I take a makeup brush and put blusher on his cheeks, followed by a dab of perfume on the top of his head. He then gets down and walks proudly through the house – tail up, whiskers spread, cooing throaty sounds. What could he be thinking? What would the neighbors think?

What does God think of us when we go to great lengths to be what we're not? Like Pookey, have we surrounded ourselves too long with those who differ greatly from us when it comes to our true values and principles? Or, like Sparkey, do we cover ourselves with pretensions or false appearances to build up our own egos?

The Bible teaches us that to grow and mature in our faith we should surround ourselves with others who are faithful. And we're told that God loves a pure heart, without a pretentious, self-centered attitude. Unlike these eccentricities of Pookey and Sparkey, I think we're meant to accept ourselves just the way God made us. After all, God, in His infinite wisdom, made us that way for a reason – as He made the whole world filled with its beautiful diversity.

Pookey and Sparkey, for all their funny, endearing quirkiness, were basically still true to their own inherent natures. And each was always convinced of her or his own natural beauty. Should we be less wise and less appreciative than these two of God's creatures?

Be assured – you are beautiful and God loves you . . . just the way you are.

WITH APPRECIATION...

Throughout this book, no humans are mentioned by name – only the animals are identified; this is, after all, their book. However, there were many human individuals involved in and important to its development. I would like to acknowledge and thank a few of them here.

Some of the preceding stories refer to "my best (human) friend." This is a man named Barry Doss. Barry has been my friend, mentor, and employer for more than 26 years. When I shared my first few stories with him, he immediately saw the potential of gathering them into a book. And, from then on, he contributed vastly to its development.

I would also like to thank my sister, Patricia Locke. An accomplished author, Patty led by example – showing me the value of having the courage to take a chance on myself and to follow my heart.

Graphic designer Lori Fox made this book come alive with her shared vision, sensitivity, enthusiasm, and considerable talent.

In closing, there are two more acknowledgements I would like to include. First, to God, for the inspiration for this book, for the animals in my life, and for the encouragement along the way. And, finally, to all the many and varied dogs and cats in my world, without whom my life would have been woefully empty and far less interesting and meaningful.

Thank you all.

- Sparkey -